BLESSED

30-DAY DEVOTIONAL

By Evangelist Jay Parker

Dedications

First and foremost, I give Honor and Praise to our Father God who made me and loves me so much he sacrificed His son on my behalf that I may be reconciled into his family once again.

Secondly, thank you Jesus for the price you paid that I may be set free from those things that held me bound and brought from death to life in you. I am so grateful for Calvary and the blood you shed so I may be set free. Thank You Jesus

Third, I want to thank the Holy Spirit for the gifts and abilities to be able to Minister and write for Gods glory. Without His indwelling spirit I could do none of this.

Finally. To my amazing wife Valeska Parker who helps me to become a better man, father, minister, and friend every day. She has been with me through thick and thin and without her encouragement and love, I would not have thought of starting this journey. She has been my cheerleader for the last 27yrs, and I am grateful to call her my wife and my friend.

Introduction

Hello, my name is Evangelist Jay Parker, and I have been serving and running for the Lord now for over 24yrs. I have served in a few different Ministries in my walk with Christ like outreach, prison, marriage, deacons, food pantry and a few others. And while serving, I have had some amazing mentors and ministers in my life that have helped me to grow and see God for who He is. We serve and Amazing and Awesome God and I pray when you have finished this 30-day devotional that you will get to know Him for who He is also. Jesus is the King of Kings and Lord of lords and there is, nor will there ever be anyone like Him. The reason for writing this devotional is to help you see who you are in Christ and to help you live every day in that calling. I pray this book touches not just your heart but also your spirit and helps you focus on the things of God and His will for your journey. These are just a few teachings and devotionals that God has given me over the last 24yrs, and I hope they help you grow and seek God's will for your life.

There is space after each devotional for you to write down what you received from each day and what God has spoken to you through his word, So, dive into this 30-day journey and become the Man/Woman God has called you to be. I genuinely believe if you follow His Word, you will come out on the other side Blessed. We are to be doers of His word and not just hearers only. So, make a commitment to read, pray and study every day. For when you do so you will find yourself walking in the blessings of God. I love you all and I look forward to all the great testimonies. and stories about your journey ahead. God Bless and thank you for purchasing Blessed.

Day 1

It is better to be quiet and stay in His will, than to speak and need forgiveness.

O That Ye Would Hold Your Peace! And It Should Be Your Wisdom. Job 13:5-KJV

I have learned over the years in ministry that people will tend to rub you the wrong way. They will gossip, they will back-bite, and they will believe stories about you that are not based on any truth whatsoever. But, because sinners do as sinners do, that never gives you permission to act differently than what God called you to be. See the enemy knows how to push your buttons and he knows which people to use to get you out of the character of God. But we must remember to do as the Apostle Paul tells us to do in **1 Corinthians 9:27** and that is to: **Put Our Bodies Under Subjection Of The Word Of God Daily**. Now I know that this is easier said than done, but remember this, if God said it in His word, than He has given us the ability to do it. It is better to stay quiet and think before we speak rather than open our mouths and need forgiveness. The word tells us to be quick to Hear, Slow to speak and Slow to wrath **(James 1;9)**

Which means, for us to keep our peace we must remain silent and listen. I need you to understand that Peace and Joy are a gift from God and the world didn't give it, so we shouldn't allow the world to take it away. When we get a hold of this wisdom that is mentioned in the beginning scripture above, we will then begin to understand that we don't need to act as the world acts and step out of the character of God. You can walk as God has called you to walk and let the world act a fool on its own. It is your choice, which will you choose? We can function as the world functions and block our blessings, or we can walk in the anointing of God, hold our peace and let God have the final say. Today that choice is yours. I pray you choose the Anointing.

Affirmation:

Say this with me: Dear Lord, please help me to keep my peace today and to remain in your will. Help me to remember I wrestle not against people, but against the enemy that is trying to get me off course. My peace and joy come from you and you alone Lord. Give me wisdom today to fight off the enemy through your word and allow you to fight my battles, In Jesus Name. Amen:

**Notes:**

Day 2

We live in a world with a lot of Knowledge, And yet no Wisdom.

If Any Of You Lack Wisdom, Let Him Ask Of God, That Give It To All Men Liberally, And Upbraideth Not; And It Shall Be Given Him. James 1:6

We live in a world where we have all the knowledge at the tip of our fingers with cell phones, tablets, computers, and other technology. The problem is, with all the knowledge we don't have any understanding or wisdom. Now I am not saying knowledge is a terrible thing, but without the other two I mentioned, it can be extremely dangerous. See, knowledge tells you how to do something, but wisdom helps you make the decision on whether you should or should not do it. **Luke 14:28** tells us to **count the cost** before we move. That means before we take on any new endeavors, speak what is on our minds or do something in hast, think before we do so. Then we are to ask ourselves, "Is This Worth It"? That is where wisdom comes in. Without wisdom, knowledge will lead us in a directions outside of Gods plan and purpose for us. Wisdom comes from Him and seeking Him is crucial part to remaining on the path that He has laid out so we can avoid the traps of the enemy.

My Bishop once told me, before he would take on any new endeavors or projects that someone would bring to him, he would first seek God in prayer. And if that thing that was brought to him was a right now thing and he didn't have time to pray over it, he would turn it down. God gives wisdom in every decision we make if we seek him in prayer for His advice. When we bring the information that we have received to the Lord, He will give us directions and wisdom on how we should move. But when we move in just knowledge alone, we find ourselves stuck in situations that could have been avoided. We have a world moving without wisdom right now and we are heading in the wrong direction. Let us get back to seeking God for direction and save ourselves. from the headache of having to ask Him to remove us from the problem we cause ourselves because we didn't use Wisdom and seek Him in the first place.

Affirmation:

Say this with me; Father, fill me with wisdom and understanding today so I may make righteous decisions in all I say and do. Let me seek your will and use wisdom in all that I accomplish this day. Allow me to wait on you before moving into anything that might become a hindrance before me. And let me seek understanding so I may move in your will. In Jesus Name; Amen

NOTES:

Day 3

Who are You?

I Will Praise Thee: For I Am Fearfully And Wonderfully Made: Marvelous Are Thy Works: And My Soul Knoweth Right Well. Psalm 134:14 - KJV

Who are you? Take a second to think about that question. Did you answer that with what your profession is, or what duties you perform? In other words, did you say I am a schoolteacher, or I am a CEO, I am a manager, or I am a husband or a wife? Those are not who you are, that is what you do. I ask many people this question and they almost always give me the same answers. My name is such and such and I am (their profession)... Just like you may have done when I asked you in the beginning of this chapter. When asked that question the answer should always be "I am a child of the Most-High God." When we put our identity in what we do and then what we do is no longer an option, we lose who we are. In other words, if you are no longer allowed to be a teacher due to layoffs or other reasons, who you are goes away with that title. Then you must find another title to make you whole again. But when our identity is found in Christ no matter what comes and goes, we know who we are and who we belong to.

Many in this world are lost because they are looking for who they are in things of this world that don't last. And when those things fade away, they fade away also. But when you place your self-worth in the one who made you, you can guarantee that you will never lose your identity in Him. In a world full of influencer's, everyone is taking advice and allowing others to form an opinion on who they should be. But you don't take your broken-down car to the refrigerator repair person to get it fixed, correct? So why do we take our lives and try to match them against people who never created us or know of our purpose in life and expect it to work? Let us place our lives in the one who fearfully and wonderfully made us. Because He alone has called you by name, and He alone created you in His Image. You are a child of God above anything and everything else. Know who you are in Christ. Your Identity is found in Jesus.

Affirmation:

Say this with me: Lord God, you know who I am, and who You called me to be. Help me too always remember I am who you say I am, and I can do what you have anointed me to do. I am clay in your hands Lord Jesus, so mold me and make me more like you. My Identity is found in you and you alone. In Jesus Precious Name.
Amen!

Notes:

Worry will not consume me.

Can any of you add one moment to his lifespan by worrying? Matthew 6:27 – CSV

The answer to the question asked by Jesus in **Matt 6:27,** is NO! Worry doesn't add to your life, worry takes life away. It does so physically, mentally, emotionally, and spiritually. Jesus tells us in **(John 10:10), "That the enemy comes to kill, steal and destroy,"** and the way he does so is by trying to cause us to worry and doubt God. See he comes to kill your anointing, he tries to steal your joy, he tries to disrupt your peace, and he tries to destroy your faith by telling you that God can't or won't do what you asked of Him. Worry doesn't bring life, only Christ can. At the end of the Scripture **of John 10:10** Jesus states, **in Him we have life and have it much more abundantly**. In Christ worry doesn't have a place to reside. When your faith is in the living word of God, fear and worry must flee because the Truth and a lie can't reside in the same place.

Worry brings on us many more issues then what you were originally worried about. Worry will causes you to become sick and damage your mind and your body. And at times it will cause you to step out of the will of God and lean on your own understanding. . So put worry in its place and let the enemy know that worrying isn't part of the agenda for today. Then begin to pray and trust God's word when He promised in **Matt 6:33** that, **If You Seek Ye First The Kingdom of God And All His Righteousness,** All Other Things Shall Be Added Unto You. Hold on to that promise and walk in His word. For, when you are seeking God, you are letting the enemy know, you have no time to worry.

Affirmation:

Say this with me: Heavenly Father, help me to keep my eyes on You and not that which the enemy is placing before me. Remind me that worry doesn't do me any good and if I place my trust in You, I have no reason to worry in the first place. I am grateful Lord that You are in my corner and in You I shall not fail. Help me to depend on you more and worry less each and every day.
In Jesus Precious Name, Amen

**Notes:**

Day 5

His promise is Joy.

These Things I Have Spoken Unto You, That My Joy Might Remain In You, And That Your Joy Might Be Full. 1 John 1:4 KJV

For a person to be happy, they have to have something good happening. The thing is, there is always something happening, and it's not always good. What we should be reaching for is the Joy of the Lord. See, Joy isn't about what's happening. It isn't about people, places or what we have physically. Joy is knowing the giver of it and knowing what God has promised you, will not fail. Joy isn't a feeling but a gift from God to those who place their trust in His word. Jesus spoke in the scripture above and in them He says that **HIS JOY** will remain in you. Meaning it was given to you by Him and no enemy can take it away. The difference between happiness and Joy is one needs a reason to happen, and the other is because of Jesus. Joy isn't based on feelings but based on facts.

And the fact is God's word never lies. You can have joy in the midst of every storm and in the middle of every trial, if you choose to receive it. So let us stop looking for things and people to make you happy and seek the Joy of the Lord. For everything else will pass away, but the joy of the Lord will be your strength, and it will remain the same even if the situation or circumstances you face may change. There is Joy in Jesus.

Affirmation:

Say this with me: Father, teach me to find my joy in You and not in the things of this world. Fill me with Your Joy that the scripture speaks as being unspeakable. Show me that no matter what is going on in life, that Your word will remain true. I place my day in your hands, and I thank you for your Son Christ Jesus and His joy that remains in me. I trust You through it all and know you are a keeper of your word. In Jesus Name; Amen

Notes:

Day 6

A Man/Woman with no vision will always go back to their past.

Where There Is No Vision, The People Parish: But He That Keepeth The Law, Happy Is He. Proverbs 29:18

Where do you see yourself in a day, a week, a month or even a year? What vision has God given you to accomplish for His glory? These questions are ones we should be ask ourselves daily. See an Idle mind is the devil's playground. And if you are not keeping your mind on the things of God, the enemy will distract you with things from the past to make you feel as if you are missing out on what God delivered you from. And trust me, the enemy can make the past look real appealing if we focus on it for to long. Without a vision to move forward we will end up stuck where we are, doing the same daily routine yet never really growing. So many people become motionless in life because they don't see themselves doing better than they did yesterday, so they end up falling backwards into the dead things of their past that was slowly bringing destruction upon them. They then get use to the mundane and never strive to move ahead. **Proverbs 26:11** Tells us when we go back from where God brought us from, it's like a dog returning to his own vomit.

This is why a vision from God about the calling on your life is so important. Then once it is given to us, we must do as it says said in **Habakkuk 2:2** and write it down so we can see it daily and run with it. You are made for more than just living day to day doing the same old thing and yet getting nowhere. God created you to make His name glorious and to have a much more abundant and fruit filled life in Him. So ask the Holy Spirit to show you how to do so, then write it down and start taking steps to head in the direction of your God given purpose. God has a plan and purpose for you. Seek that purpose and continue looking forward in Christ. Remember don't look back or get distracted by the things of the enemy, for greater days are yet to come.

Affirmation:

Say this with Me: Lord God, help me to find my purpose in You. I know You created me for more than just living day to day. Help me to keep my eyes on the prize and to continue pressing towards the goals You have laid out for me. When I grow weak Lord, strengthen me and when I get weary, carry me Lord. Show me my purpose for Your will so that I may represent You fully. Renew Your vision within me and grant me the wisdom and anointing to complete it. In Jesus Name: Amen

Notes:

Day 7

Get in alignment

You Lust And Do Not Have. You Murder And Covet And Cannot Obtain. You Fight And War. Yet You Do Not Have Because You Do Not Ask. You Ask And Do Not Receive, Because You Ask Amiss, That You May Spend It On Your Peasures.
James 4:2-3

Many are waiting on their blessings, but God is waiting on them to get in alignment to receive them. Now before you go and think that I am speaking about financial blessing, and I am doing the whole prosperity gospel thing, hold on. When I am speak of blessings, I speak of Breakthroughs, Deliverances, New Anointing's, Promotions, Healing and yes at times Financial Blessings See all these things are gifts and promises of God toward His people who are called by His name and walk according to His purpose. Now why are they Blessings? They are blessings because we don't deserve them. They are benefits given because of the sacrifice of Christ on the Cross alone and not because of our abilities or talent. But many don't receive all of Gods benefits because we are not in a receiving position. What I mean by this is, they are not in alignment with Gods word or will. See God is not going to give you something until you are mature enough to handle it.

God knows if He gives you something too early it may cause a hindrance in your walk. I have seen people receive homes, relationships, healing, and breakthroughs, only to walk away from God after obtaining them and end up in a bad place because they seeked the blessings more than they seeked God. The scripture above says, **"That You Ask Amiss",** meaning you are asking with the wrong motives and desires. When you ask for something of God, it should always be with the intent to use it for His glory. You are blessed to be a Blessing. But when we ask for our own lustful desires, we ask unaligned with Gods word and most likely, we will not receive it. So, today get in alignment and seek God for those things that will help you benefit the Kingdom of God. Because your breakthrough is near, the question is will you use it for Him or yourself? I pray the answer is for Him.

Affirmation:

Say this with Me: Father God, today help me to get in alignment with You and Your word so I may receive what You have for me this day. Keep me mindful that what you give Lord should be used for You and You alone. Help me to be a good steward of the blessings that I receive and when I am not Lord, correct me. I thank You for all You have already done in my life and help me get in position for what is to come next.
In Jesus Name I Pray: Amen!

Notes:

Day 8

That still and quiet and voice.

And Ye Shall Seek Me, And Find Me, When Ye Shall Search For Me With Your Whole Heart.
Jeremiah 29:13.

How many of us are waiting on a burning bush experience and missing God speaking through the quiet breeze of day? We are seeking God for guidance and then we stand waiting for the lightning bolt or earthquake to hit, not realizing that God may be moving in the silence and wanting us to stop so we can hear Him in it. Trusting God means even when we don't get the burning bush, we take Him at His word. There have been times I have asked God to show me a sign for one thing or another and couldn't hear Him because of the noise of life around me. But when I got in that quiet place and turned off the world, I heard Him clearly. It is time to get into that quiet place and seek God with your whole heart. He wants to give you directions, but He is waiting for you to sit still to receive it. Open the lines of communication with God in prayer and through the reading of His word and tune the world out with all its distractions. You will find in those moments that God was speaking the whole time, but we just couldn't hear Him because we weren't listening for that still small voice.

God is still giving direction and if we would turn off the cellphones, televisions and computers and listen with our Spirits and not just our minds. God will show us His plans and purpose for our lives and reveal Himself to you. At times you may hear Silences, but that doesn't mean no. Those silent times mean, get busy doing what God has called you to do in His word until He answers. God is an on-time God and when you are in a place ready to receive, God will do exceedingly and abundantly of all you can ask or think. Turn off the noise and listen in your Spirits for that still small voice. God is still giving guidance today. Get connected and trust His word when He said "We Can Be Confident That He Hears Our Prayers. **(1 John 5;14-15)**

Affirmation:

Say this with me: Lord, help me to hear Your voice when I seek You and to turn off all the distractions around me. In a life full of busyness, help me to stop and listen to for when You are speaking. You said your sheep know your voice and another they shall not follow. Teach me to know Your voice Lord so I may move in the direction You would have me to go. Teach us to hear You in the quiet times Father, so when I seek You with my whole heart, I can hear You clearly. In Jesus Name, Amen!

Notes:

Day 9

The other side of obedience.

If My People Which Are Called By My Name, Shall Humble Themselves And Pray, And Seek My Face, And Turn From Their Wicked Ways: Then Will I Hear From Heaven, And Forgive Their Sins, And Will Heal Their Lands.
2 Chronicles 7:14

The scripture above tells us when we are obedient and do as God has asked, He will hear and carry out what He has promised. See many only want to do one or two of the items listed in the first half of the scripture and then we expect God to do **ALL** that He promised in the second half. He tells us to Humble Ourselves, Pray, Seek His Face, And Turn/Repent from our wicked ways, yet many want to Seek & Pray and forget the other two directives, and then expect God to Hear, to Forgive and to Heal. We must understand that it is on the other side of our obedience that we will see the full manifestation of Gods true power in our lives. When we don't just select what we want to do, and do all He has asked us to do, that is when we find the true blessings in our walk with Him. The scriptures are not there to pick and choose which to follow and not follow. Let us understand, Ninety-nine and a half won't do.

God always keeps His word/promises, yet it is up to us to walk in them and carry out His directives. Just like the kids game from back in the day called Hopscotch. See, if you followed the directions, stayed in the lines, and only put your foot down on the correct boxes all the way through to the end of the board, you won the game. But the first time you stepped outside the box or put two feet down when you weren't supposed to, you lost. God has given us the directions to live by so we may live an abundant life in Him. And if we do as God has asked, we will see His Glory prevail in our lives. So let us not step outside the box or cross the line but let us complete the task at hand. For when we do, we will see His promises come forth and we will walk into our blessings on the other side of our obedience.

__Affirmation__

Say This With Me: Father God, help me today to follow Your whole word and not just pick and choose what fits me. Help me to be obedient to You, not just in the easy moments but in the tough ones too. Lord, I believe in Your promises and trust You at your word. Help me to follow Your word in all aspects of life. So, I may live a blessed and peaceable life in You. In Jesus Name: Amen

Notes:

Day 10

God is my strength.

And He Said To Me, "My Grace Is Sufficient For You, For My Strength Is Made Perfect In Weakness: 2 Corinthians 12:9

You may be one of many people who are battling in one or two areas of their lives right now and feel as if the battle is getting the best of them. Whether their battles be with Sin, Addictions, Depression, Physical, Mental or Spiritual warfare, we find ourselves becoming weak and overwhelmed in our fight to stay right in the Lord. But today, I want to remind you that the fight isn't yours. The battles have already been won because of the Cross that Christ bared for you and me, and we are already victorious. Let me tell you about three characteristic of God that I have learned over the years. **1. God does not fail. 2. God does not lie** and **3. God does not change His mind**. Because of these characteristics, Gods promises remain true today. He promise His Grace is sufficient in your weakness and it is. So, in weakness we must lean on that Grace and seek His strength when ours just won't make it. God is the same Yesterday, Today and Forever and His Grace and Mercy are new every morning.

Hebrews 12:2: tells us to **Look Unto Jesus Who Is The Author And Finisher Of Our Faith**... **Psalms 121:1**: tells us. **To Look Towards The Hills From Which Comes Our Help, For My Help Comes From The Lord**. The hill that is spoken of is the Hill of Calvary. The Author that is spoken of is Christ Jesus who died on the Cross on that hill. It is in His sacrifice that we find our strength to overcome our weaknesses, our faults, and failures. Not in ourselves but in God's Grace. So, remember today that the battle you are facing has already been won. Then stand in the Victory of God's living Word and remember you are strong even in the midst of weakness. Not because of you, but because of the strength of Christ that resides in You. You are victorious in Christ Jesus. You are a conquer and an overcomer. Get up Kings Kid and stand tall.

Affirmation:

Say This With Me: Lord God, remind me daily that I am victorious in You. Help me to remember in those weak times my strength is found in You. You are the Author and Finisher of my faith, and I know You did not bring me this far to leave me. Let me be mindful that even when I am weak Lord, in You I Am Strong. In Jesus Precious Name: Amen.

Notes:

Day 11

What can man do when God is on my side?

Be Not Afraid Of Their Faces: For I AM With Thee To Deliver Thee, Saith The LORD. Jeremiah 1:8

When we are placed into positions by God, whether on the job or in the church, we need to understand that we have the full authority and ability of God to fulfill that calling. We need to learn to live for an Audience of One and that one is Christ Jesus. We get so focused on what others think, feel, and say about us and we never really walk in our full potential in Christ hoping not to offend others. We cannot please people all the time, nor is it our job to do so. People are always going to talk, so when they do, let's give them Jesus to talk about. God has placed you in the position that you are in to bring His name glory. Yet we remain silent and scared to walk in that authority because of how others may feel and think about us. But when you begin to realize that you are where God wants you to be for His purpose, not because of your ability or inability, then and only then can walk in the power of Gods authority that is given to you.

Just know when you do step up, people will smirk, look down on you, and even question what you are doing. or how did you get there? But in the midst of all that, stand tall and **Be Not Afraid**. For God did not place you there to make Himself look foolish. But He placed you there to make His name glorious. Once you begin to move in that anointing, the Great I AM is with you. He will bring forth in you, all He wants to accomplish for you. So, stay focused and walk tall. God called you there and God will lead you through. So, walk in your calling and know God is on your side. And When God before you, nothing or no one can come against you.

Affirmation

Say this with Me: Lord Jesus, help me live for you today and walk out my calling. The Holy Spirit guide me in the way I should go and remind me who I am in you. Fill me with wisdom, knowledge, understanding and boldness to do what you have ordained me to do. Don't let me lose sight of you as I stand in the place you have called me to. Let me glorify you alone in all I say and do. In Jesus Name: Amen

Notes:

Day 12

Don't let a bad 5 minutes ruin your 24 hours.

For Our Light Affliction, Which Is But For A Moment, Is Working For Us A Far More Exceeding And Eternal Weight Of Glory, 2 Corinthians 4:17

We are all given 24 hours daily to fulfill the will of God, and in that 24 hours we find ourselves allowing a bad 5 minutes to throw us off course and mess us the entire day. We sometimes magnify that one moment and allow it to become bigger than it actually may be. Then we allow our thoughts to bring us down a rabbit hole that takes our focus off of the job at hand and that in turn ruins everything else before us.. We can't see the blessings of God because we are more focused on what happen beforehand and we lose track of what we were called to do, so we end up missing out on what God may have planned or what He is doing in that moment. See, this is what the enemy does. He is the author of confusion, and if he can get you to focus on that issue, he can get you to stop focusing on Gods calling. Let us learn to brush off the bad moments just as quick as they come, and then get back to focusing and the other 23 hours and 55 minutes of the day. In fact, that issue can be a learning moment to help you see Gods glory in it, if you allow it to be. I usually take moments like those to show me how far God has brought me.

See, moments like that in the past, I would have blown up and lost my cool over them. But now I know how to shake it off and move on from them and continue on in the battle. This helps me to see the Glory of God in my life and reminds me of where God has brought me from. It also helps me to remember what the enemy meant for evil; God works it out for His good. So, the next time a issues pops up, ask God how can you glorify Him in it. Remember this is just a stumbling block that was placed by the enemy who is trying to throw us off course. and then realize like everything else, this too shall pass. Brush it off solider and move forward in Christ for there are other battles ahead. Don't let a bad 5min ruin your whole day.

Affirmation:

Say this with Me: Holy Spirit, keep me to be mindful that the enemy comes to throw me off course and that those stumbling blocks only succeed if I allow them to. As I go through this day let me continue to hold my peace in every battle I may face and help me to lift my voice in praise no matter what comes my way. I will reject the negative thoughts that try to consume my mind and replace them with your promises. Your glory shall be revealed in every situation that rears its ugly head against me. Remind me of this very truth every day. Thank you, Lord, for answering me today, In Jesus Precious Name: Amen.

NOTES:

Day 13

Elevation comes from above and not below.

For Promotion Cometh Neither From The East Or The West, Nor From The South. But God Is The Judge: He Putteth Down One, And Setteth Up Another. Psalm 75:6

Whether it be at work, in church or life in general, stop looking for man to put you in places that only God can bring you. We are seeking the attention of others, whether they are our bosses, pastors, friends, or family, in hopes that it will put us in places that we feel we belong. But it is God who gives out those positions and until we are ready Mentally and Spiritually to be placed in them, we remain where we are. When it is time for you to get to a place God has for you, and He opens that door, there is no man can deny you that position. What God has for you is for you and our job is to let our light shine for His glory until He prepares us to step into that anointing. I have seen many people force their way into places for which they were not ready and a little while later they walked away from them. Reason being if God doesn't open it for you, it will not last. So don't get upset when others move ahead or get something you believed you deserved. In fact, praise God for them and with them as they receive their increase.

Because our Father in Heaven keeps good records and He sees your heart. When it is your time, the gates of hell can't even prevail against you or stop you from your elevation or promotion from God. So, until God makes a way, praise him in advance. Because while you are out here looking for good, God is working to give you His absolute best. Always remember not all that glitters is gold and it is quite possible God didn't allow you to have what you wanted because He knew there may have been price too high to pay to have it. God's gifts come without repentance and when He sets you up, no man can take you down.

Affirmation

Say This with Me: Lord God, teach me to wait on You. Help me not to rush your plans, but to be obedient to your word while I wait for my opportunity. My elevation comes from you, so prepare me mentally and spiritually for what lies ahead. Help me to celebrate when others are raised up and understand that what is for me is for me. Help me realize You will open that door in your time Lord. But until then Father, I will praise You in the Hallway. Let me see beyond my desire and be patient for Your will. You know what is best for me, so I will praise you while I wait. In Jesus Name: Amen.

NOTES:

Day 14

And Yet We Still Question God.

And Jesus Answered And Said Unto Them, Have Faith in God
Mark 22:11

How is it that we trust the word of the people around us who have failed us repeatedly, yet we don't trust God who is batting a thousand when it comes to His promises? God has fulfilled every promise He has ever made and every covenant He has spoken, He has kept. But repeatedly we continue to doubt Him at His word and believe He can't or won't do it for us. In the scripture of **Mark 9:24**, a father came to Jesus seeking healing for his son. Jesus asked him the question **"do you believe I can heal him"? and the man answered, "I Believe Lord, Help Thou My Unbelief."** The issue to the question in the beginning, was a mindset thing. See the Father knew in his heart Jesus could heal, and he believed enough that he went searching for Him. But His mind was trying to tell him differently. See our minds are a battlefield for the enemy. In them he causes doubt, confusion, worry, fear, anxiety and distractions. Our heart knows God can do it, but we lean on our own understanding and don't see how or why God would do it on our behalf. Answer: He responds to our Faith in Him

Mark tells us to Have Faith in God. That means to suspend what you think you know and walk by faith. The reason we trust others before we trust God is because they are right in front of us. But God who we don't see physically is more dependable than anyone we can see. The word tells us to "Hide His Word in Our Hearts", and I believe He said put it there because our minds won't keep them for long. Scripture also says, "You Must Believe with Your Heart", meaning opening your heart to the possibilities of God, So, when you get into doubt mode you can search your heart for the word that God has given you and ask Him to help you with that unbelief. Because unlike man God cannot fail, but it's the doubt in our minds will cause us to search elsewhere. Today, remove all doubt because faith says, **God Can**!

Affirmation :

Say This with Me: Lord, I take You at Your word, Please help me with my unbelief. When doubt and worry begin to flood my mind, bring to remembrance your promises for me. When I grow weary Lord, remind me of the testimonies of my past and all you have brought me through. You are the same God now as back then, help me to walk in this truth. I trust You and You alone Father. Cause me not to lean on my own understanding, but to walk in the promises of your word. In Jesus Name I Pray: Amen.

NOTES:

Day 15

It is time to work it out.

Wherefore My Beloved, As Ye Have Aways Obeyed, Not As In My Presence Only, But Now Much More In My Absence, Work Out Your Own Salvation With Fear And Trembling. Philippians 2:1

There are times when you we find ourselves standing and waiting for Jesus to do something on our behalf that He has already given us the authority to do. We are dealing in areas in our lives that Christ already proclaimed victory for on the Cross when He said, **"It Is Finished."** We have a tough time letting go of sins, hurts, pains and un-forgiveness of self and others that God has asked us to let go of. God gave us the authority to conquer sin and death. Yet we seek Gods face on a regular to take away the sin we wrestle with. In the meantime, Jesus is sitting on the thrown asking when will you use the authority given you, by me to put that thing down? Christ is not going to place Himself on that Cross again so you can defeat sin. He has already conquered it and gave you the ability to conquer it also, when He proclaimed in His word that He has Given you Power **(Luke 10:19)** But many never overcome sin, because we never use the power given. But the Scriptures tells us to Obey and Work. Meaning obey what He taught and work it out in action. This means telling your flesh no and doing as the Apostle Paul said and Put Your Flesh Under The Subjection Of God's Word Daily, **(1 Corinthians 9:26)**.

This means always fighting the temptation of sin in your mortal body and mind and believing God when He said **"Submit Yourselves Therefore To God And Resist The Enemy, He Will Flee, (James 4:7)**. You can overcome sin, but it is going to take trusting in Christ and doing some work on your behalf. This means rebuking the enemy, fighting your flesh and your thoughts, and submitting to what God has said by focusing on His word and praying daily for your deliverance. The more you work it out, the easier it becomes to resist it. Listen, you can't rebuke the enemy with whom you are dancing with. It is time to find a new dance partner. God has made you an overcomer through His Son Jesus Christ. Once you start dancing in the steps He has laid out in His word, you will then begin to overcome the sin you are in.

Affirmation:

Say This with Me: Father, help me to see that I am an overcomer. I no longer want to dabble in the things that keep me from you. Jesus died and arose on my behalf so I can be set free from the shame of sin. Help me to put my body under subjection of Your word and walk as You have called me to. I thank You Jesus for giving the authority to walk in freedom in you. I also thank you for your forgiveness for all those times I fell short. Lord and lead unto the path of your righteousness. In Jesus Name I pray: Amen

Notes:

Day 16

His healing is waiting on you.

He Was Wounded For Our Transgressions, He Was Bruised For Our Iniquities, The Chastisement Of Our Peace Was Upon Him, And By His Stripes We Are Healed. Isaiah 53:5

Your guilt and shame no longer belong to you. Yet we continue living in it. See your guilt and shame was defeated on Calvary by the Blood of the Lord Jesus Christ. Yet we continue to stay locked in our past because we somehow believe in our hearts that there is no way God forgave me for this, But He Did! The thing is, His healing depends on you. It depends on whether you will decide to receive His forgiveness and release the guilt and shame to Him, or will you keep carrying it around on your own. God will not work on something you refuse to relinquish to Him. You have to make that choice to give it up. He tells us to **"Cast Our Cares On Him" 1 Peter 5:7.** Meaning anything and everything that is in your heart that is taking up space from Him. Every hurt, pain, disappointment, failure and flaw we are to give over to the Lord. When we do, He will then replace those things with Joy, Peace, Love, Forgiveness, Restoration, Deliverance, Grace, Mercy, and Healing. But again, it depends on you. You must open your heart to release to Him and then open it again to receive from Him.

You have been healed of those past mistakes and failures. You are healed of those past hurts and pains. Jesus bore them all back there on Calvary, so you don't have to bear them now. But you have to let them go. You must forgive yourself and others, you must stop beating yourself up for your past. God said, **"AS Far As The East Is From The West, He Has Removed Our Transgressions From Us" Psalm 103:12.** God isn't holding on to them, so why should you. It is time to let that thing that the Holy Spirit has placed in your mind while you were reading this, go. Your healing can begin today, but it is up to you to walk in that promise. Christ paid the ultimate sacrifice so you can be set free. It is similar to paying a check at a dinner that someone else has already paid for. We wouldn't do that, so why are we holding on to things God said He has freed us from? The guilt and shame are no longer yours. Your freedom is in the Lord. It's up to you to claim it.

Affirmation

Say This with Me: Holy Spirit, show me how to walk in the freedom that is found in you. I am no longer the owner of my guilt and shame. Help me to learn to forgive myself and others and walk in the newness of life that you have given me through the Blood of your son Jesus Christ. I lay down all those things that are stopping me from walking in freedom. I thank You for Your sacrifice, Lord and for setting me free. I choose that Freedom today that is found in you. in Jesus Name Precious Name: Amen

<u>Notes:</u>

Day 17

I no longer own that.

**If the Son Shall Make You Free, Ye Shall Be Free Indeed.
John 8:36**

The Enemy would have you believe that when you come to Christ that fear, worry, anxiety, depression, sickness, and generational curses still belong to you. But John 8:36 says you are set free. It is what we believe and what we listen to that makes the difference on whether you are changed, or you will remain the same. See the enemy will continue to call you by your past. He wants you to believe is, that the decision you made to follow Christ really didn't make a difference or a meaningful change in your life. But **2 Corinthians 5:17** tells **us that you are a new creation in Christ Jesus.** Let us remember that Jesus said to us just as He said to the man sitting at the Temple, **We Are Made Whole, Sin No More: (John 5:14).** When you believe that Jesus is who he says He is and that God will do what he says He will do, you will then understand that the old you with the old ways no longer has control over you. God has given you a new way of thinking, a different perspective and a new outlook on life. When you walk in His word and trust in His promises, we begin to see that we don't have to remain the way we are.

When you give your life to Him and trust Him at His word, your views become different, your speech begins to change and our outlook on life becomes more focused, and your past is washed away. So, when the enemy tries to remind you of your past, remind him of his future and then proclaim that your future is now in Christ, and you are no longer who you use to be. Today is a new day, with new opportunities and God has made a way for you and directed your steps. So don't look back and dwell on what has been. Move in your destiny and trust God for the journey. Leave your past behind and give those things that had you bound to God. For today the Son has made you free and in Him you are free indeed. You are no longer a slave to sin and shame.

Affirmation

Say This with Me: Holy Spirit, help me to walk in the freedom that is found in you. Remind me to put the enemy on notice every time that he tries and bring up my past, that I no longer reside there. I lay down the doubt, fear, anxiety, guilt and shame of the enemy, because they no longer belong to me. I thank You for Your sacrifice Jesus and the price that was paid for my freedom in you. I give you all the Praise Honor and Glory this day. In Jesus Mighty Name I pray: Amen

NOTES:

Day 18

No matter what you know, remain teachable.

***Shew Me thy ways, O'Lord: teach Me Thy Paths. Lead
Me In Thy Truth, And Teach Me.
Psalm 25:4-5.***

My Bishop, Clarence E Lassiter, would always say these
three words to me, "Always Remain Teachable." The
reason he would say this is because we have the
propensity to think we know everything, and we can make
our own way. Yet this is so far from the truth. Every day
we have an opportunity to learn new things in Christ and
understand what He means when He says, "**His Ways and
Thoughts are not our ways and thoughts" (Isaiah
55:8-9).** There is so much we must learn to move away
from in our past thinking when we decided to live for
Christ. Our old ways of thinking and moving does not line
up to what God has for us in our newness of life. This
means we must be ready to submit to His teachings and
begin to re-learn all that we thought we knew.
**Proverbs 12:15 tells us, "A Fool Is Right In His Own
Eyes; Be He That Harken Unto Counsel Is Wise."**
Remaining teachable is a big step towards wisdom. God
can use anyone at any time to teach you who He is and
what He wants from you. But if you place God in a box
and only look for lessons from certain people or only want
to learn certain things, then you miss Gods wisdom.

The word tells us, **To Study To Show Thy Self Approved: 2 Timothy 2:15.** We should always strive to learn, improve, and grow in Christ. God is always speaking to us in his word and showing Himself daily in different areas in our lives. We should be willing and able to see, listen and learn the lessons that are coming our way. Today don't look at life as if there is nothing new to achieve, accomplish or conquer. If Christ has given you the breath of life today, then there is something new to learn. His word is alive, and He is always teaching us daily the good from bad and right from wrong. Let us open up our bibles and then get ready to see the lessons throughout the day. Because when you are in a position to learn something, you will learn. Remain Teachable and receive.

Affirmation:

Say This with Me: Lord, teach me your ways and lead me in the way you would have me to go. Help me to receive from you the lessons in life you want me to learn. Your thoughts are not my thoughts, nor are your ways my ways Lord. So, lead me in your ways and teach me your thoughts so I may live for You and You alone. In Jesus Name: Amen.

Notes:

Day 19

Quiet in the storm

And He Arose, And Rebuked The Wind, And Said Unto The Sea, Peace Be Still. And The Winds Ceased, And There Was A Great Calm.
Mark 4:39

At times it may feel as if the storm may never die down. It seems as if one thing after another has come up against you and there is no end in sight. But in the midst of all the turmoil, Jesus is still there with you. He is the quiet in the storm, when you begin to focus on Him and not the rain and the winds. He is able to make peace in the midst of a chaotic situation and bring you out of the floods and strong currents. But this only happens when we place our focus on Christ and Christ alone. See we seem to speak about the issues and circumstances more than we focus on the promises of God, we get discouraged and begin to waver in our faith. We keep our minds on the issue instead of God, causes that thing we are focused on to begin to seem bigger than it really are. Jesus Name is above every other name and when we call on His name and place our eyes on Him, we see that He is the way-maker, when there seems to be no way out. When you take a look back on past testimonies of what God has done for you, you can see that those things that you worried about back then really weren't as devastating as we thought they were.

The same is true about the things we face now. We are more than conquerors and our testimonies of Gods goodness has proven this repeatedly. He has brought peace into every storm we have faced, and in this storm, He will do the same. Get your eyes back on Jesus and tell the enemy this too shall pass. The enemy may have caused the storm to come up against you. But Jesus is standing in the middle of it saying, **"PEACE BE STILL"**, and because so the flood waters will never overtake you nor will God allow you to be destroyed. The Lord is our peace, and we need to call on the Jesus before, during and even after the storm. For when you call on the name of Jesus, the storm must cease and in Him your peace is restored.

Affirmation

Say This with Me: Father, help me to find my peace in you. Remind me Lord that you have made me an overcomer. You said in your words that I am more than a conqueror in you. Lord, I ask that you help me to hear your voice when the winds roar and let not the waves of life take me under. Let your voice be louder than the storm in my life so I can hear from you clearly. You are my peace Lord and in you I find my refuge. Remind me when I feel overwhelmed by this very thing. Thank you, Father, for always keeping me. In Jesus Name I Pray: Amen.

Notes:

Day 20

Better check the price tag.

For Which Of You, Intending To Build A Tower, Sitteth Not Down First, And Counteth The Cost, Whether He Have Sufficient To Finish It? Luke 14:28

We have heard that saying in times past that we must pay the cost to be the boss. And Lord knows, that saying is so true. There is a cost to taking on new endeavors, roles, or opportunities. But there is something else that also comes at a cost. That is our actions, conversations, and the moves we make in everyday life. Before we do anything, say anything, or move in any direction, we should count the cost of what this action may bring or not bring, and then check to see if it will be a help or a hindrance to our walk in Christ. It is said that sin will take you further than you intended to go, keep you longer than you intended to stay and cost you more than you intended to pay. So, before you say what you feel, count the cost. Before you go where you shouldn't go, count the cost, and before You act out and do what you know in your heart you should not do, count the cost. Ask yourself, is this worth my time, my energy, and my peace? Will me saying or doing this add or subtract to my life and the life of those around me? And if so, is that addition or subtraction worth it? And most important of all, will this bring God glory in any way? See, we must check the price tag before we buy that headache, disturbance, chaos. We should ask ourselves, is it going to cost me more than I am willing to pay, if I were to say or do what is on my mind? We will give an account for everything that is said and done in our mortal bodies. So let us give an account of the good we have done and not the bad. Everything comes at a price. It is our job to count the cost and make sure it's not more than we want to pay. If it does not edify yourself and those around you and bring glory to God, then it is not worth doing. Remember the saying, "The road to hell was paved with good intentions." The intentions may seem good, but always count the cost.

Affirmation:

Say This with Me: As I count the cost of everything I say and do Lord, help me to remember that all I say and do is for you. Teach me to hold my peace when my flesh says otherwise. Help me to remember that I am your vessel here to bring You glory. Give me directions and teach me so that I may go when you say go speak when you say speak. Remind me to count the cost every day of my actions and to understand that I represent you always. I want to remain in your will for my life, because in your will I find my strength, my peace, my joy, and my direction. So, remind me each and every day to count the cost in all I do. In Jesus Name: Amen.

Notes:

Day 21

Today I Chose Peace

Depart From Evil And Do Good. Seek Peace And Pursue It
Psalm 34:14

We seek many things in life like a career, a relationship, financial status and objects. But did you know that God told you to seek Peace and not just seek it but to Pursue it? To pursue something means to follow it, keep track of it, or better yet chase it down. God tells us this because many times during the day for one reason or another we tend lose our peace and relinquish our joy due to situations that may arise around us. We allow people to cause us to lose our peace and then allow the enemy to wreak havoc in our hearts and minds, as we begin to slide back into our fleshly nature. But the word of God tells us to **depart from evil and seek peace**, and when we seek peace, we seek Jesus. When we pursue His will and His Way we pursue peace. **Matthew 5:9** states **Blessed Are The Peacemakers: For They Shall Be Called The Children Of God.** As a child of God, we are to be seeking peace, pursuing peace and making peace every opportunity we have. That means having a made-up mind that, no matter how another may act towards me, I will continue chasing after Christ. Then once you have a made-up mind that today nothing, nor anyone shall take your peace, the enemies tricks don't prevail.

Seek peace every day in every situation you face in your workplace, in your homes and even in the marketplace. Never let another person take you out of the character of Christ. **Job 13:15** says **"Though He Slay Me, Yet I Will Trust Him: But I Will Maintain My Own Ways Before Him"**. People are going to do what they do and act the way they act. But we must always Maintain Christ-like ways before them and God and pursue peace. That means showing the Love of God even in the tough times. So, find your peace in Jesus, Chase your Peace in Jesus and hold on to your Peace in Jesus and never relinquish it. As the word says, Blessed are those who do so.

Affirmation:

Say This with Me: Heavenly Father, I thank you for my peace today. I know you sent your Son on my behalf and my peace is found in Him. No matter what comes my way today, help me not to relinquish my peace or give up my joy that is found in you. Help me to seek peace, hold my peace and continually throughout the day to pursue my peace in every situation that may arise. Remind me Father. that my peace isn't found in the things of this world and because of this nothing in this world can take it from me unless I give it up willingly. Keep me in remembrance of this as I go through my day, In Jesus Name: Amen

NOTES:

Day 22

**Let the word show you the blemishes and then work to
fix them.**

*But Be Doers Of The Word And Not Hearers Only, Deceiving
Yourselves. Because if Anyone Is A Hearer Of The Word And Not A
Doer, He Is Like A Man Looking At His Own Face In The Mirror, For
He Looks At Himself, And Goes Away, And Immediately Forget
What Manner Of Man He Was. James 1:22-24*

God's word isn't here for us to read as a good novel or to
listen to like it's some catchy lyrics from a song. It is here
to help us change and become the men and women that
God intended for us to be. The word is a mirror into the
heart and mind, and it will show you where and how you
are falling short in Christ. Just as a glass mirror shows you
your blemishes and flaws, the bible is a spiritual mirror, or
one can say a spiritual barometer that shows you where
you are falling short in the things of God. It reveals the
issues in your heart that are hindering your growth in
Christ. So, after you read it, apply it to your life and walk
as it says to walk. Because it will help you change for the
better. **Romans 8:1** says **That there is no Condemnation
to those in Christ Jesus.** So, when studying the word
don't look at it as a condemnation, or as God coming down
on you.

But look at it as God showing you were to tighten some things up in your walk so you may see more glorious days ahead. Every promise in God's word for you will be fulfilled and He will continue to supply every provision you need to succeed and every convent found in His teachings shall be kept on your behalf, but It is up to us whether we line up with His word to be in place to receive them. So let us look into the mirror/bible daily, so He can touch up those blemishes that are keeping us from reaching our full potential in Him. For as it is written in **Psalm 119: 105, They Word is a lamp unto my feet and a light unto my path**. Let his Word/Mirror guide your path into His righteousness always.

Affirmation:

Say this with Me: Lord God show me daily those things in my heart and mind that are not pleasing to you. As I seek your word speak to me in the areas of my life where I fall short of your calling. Give me the strength to overcome those things that are holding me back and show me those things or people that are a hindrance and not a help to my spiritual growth. I thank you for your correction and the guidance You have given to help me become who you have called me to be. Continue to work on me as I follow you and Lord. In Jesus Precious Name: Amen.

Notes:

Day 23

This is temporary. Hold on to God's promises.

For I reckon that the sufferings of this present time are not worthy to be compared with the glory which shall be revealed in us.
Romans 8:18

The enemy would have you to believe that what is going on in your life right now is a permanent thing. He would have you believe that this issue at home or at work, or the issues in your health, finances, relationships, marriage, family life or even in your own mind is a battle that can't be won. So, he tries to convince you to just give up and accept your defeat. Well **Roman's 8:18** tells us differently. Because these things we face are only temporary and for the present moment. Those who are in Christ have already won the battle because of the victory given when they took a look in the Grave and seen, that Christ had risen and the tomb was empty. He has already won the battle and every situation we face must come under the subjection of God's word. In His word, it says, His Glory shall be revealed. So, let us always remember that this situation we may be facing may feel as if it's the end, but it isn't because God has the final say.

You just have to overcome and push through this present time event and trust God. Revelation 12:11 Says: And They Overcame Him By The Blood Of The Lamb And The Word Of Their Testimony. The Testimonies we stand on today is, **John 19:30**: Christ said **"It Is Finished"** and **Romans 8:18:** God said His Glory Shall Be Revealed. So, in every situation and circumstance, to hold on and trust God. Continue to press through today towards better days ahead. Because every promise in God is true and Amen. Because God Does Not Lie.

Affirmation:

Say this with me: Heavenly Father, I trust in Your word and believe in your promises. Help me to stay focused on the things of you in the midst of my battles and storms. Let me not listen to the lies of the enemy who is telling me it's over. But let me hear that still small voice from you that tells me to continue to push through. Thank you for reminding me that this trial I face is only temporary and that Your word is forever. Strengthen me to stand strong and know that Your glory will be revealed though it all. In Jesus Name: Amen

Notes:

Day 24

Your Morning is closer than you think.

For His Anger is But For A Moment, His Favor Is For Life; Weeping Way Endure For A Night, But Joy Comes In The Morning. Psalm 30:5

We have cried, we have reasoned with God, we have prayed and some of us may have even gotten angry and fed up. But I pray that none has given up. So many times, people will give up just before their breakthrough. They stop fighting, throw in the towel, quit on God and sometimes, even life itself. But this is exactly what the enemy would have us to do. He doesn't want you to see that your breakthrough is near, so he turns the pressure up to maximum, in hopes you will quit and give in. But God says that your weeping is over and that your Joy is here. The thing is, when will you choose to use it? Jesus is that joy and your morning is now. So, when you get to a place when you are sick and tired of being sick and tired, wipe your tears and claim your joy in Christ Jesus. His words say in **Proverbs 18:10: That The Name Of The Lord Is A Strong Tower. The Righteous Run Into It And They Are Saved.** Jesus Christ is that strong tower where we can find refuge in the moment of pain and weeping.

Sorrow is only a temporary thing, but Gods promise of Shelter is eternal and never fails. Knowing this should bring us joy and the will to want to carry on through every circumstance we face. So before admitting defeat and letting the enemy have the victory over your life, let us instead run to the living word of God and find the shelter, refuge and strength we need to be able to navigate through the storms ahead. Never forget that **1 Corinthians 15:57; says, Thanks Be To God Which Gives Us The Victory.** Right now, the victory is yours. Even though you may not feel it, you still have the right in Christ to walk in it. Jesus already made a way, walk Victorious

Affirmation:

Say this with Me: Father God, I thank you for the victory. I thank you, Lord, for the Strength and refuge that I find only in you. I am grateful Father for the sacrifice of your Only Son Christ Jesus that has won the victory on calvary for me. On those days I struggle to remember this Lord remind me in your words. Help me to keep focused on you alone in every circumstance I may face. You are my strong tower and my shelter Lord and in you I will stand. Thank you for wiping away every tear. In Jesus Name: Amen

Notes:

Day 25

A Reminder Of Who You Are.

But Ye Are a Chosen Generation, A Royal Priesthood, A Holy Nation,, A Peculiar People; That Ye Should Show Forth The Praises Of Him Who Called You Out Of The Darkness And Into The Marvelous Light;
1 Peter 2:9

Life has a way of beating you down to the point where you forget who you are and to whom you belong. It can steal your belief, kill your joy, and rob you of your peace. But today I have come to remind you to lift your head and brush off your shoulder's warrior, because you are the child of the King of kings and the Lord of lords, who was made to conquer for Christ. Scripture says: **But thou, O LORD, art a shield for me; my glory, and the lifter up of mine head. Psalm 3:3.** Two words that should never go together is Defeated-Christian. See, Jesus already conquered every battle that you may be facing today, and He is the lifter of your head. So, you don't have to walk slumped over in a defeated position wondering if you will make it through this trail. You are a Kings kid and because you are, you have the promises of the inheritance left to you in Christ Jesus. That means every weapon has been given to you to walk in Victory. But it is up to you whether you choose to use those weapons, or you choose to allow the enemy to continually to beat you down.

God has given you His word to speak over your situations. He has given you the ability to pray and seek His face in the midst of the strongest temptations, He has given you the ability to praise Him even in the midst of the toughest battles. And He has given you the name of His son Christ Jesus which is the name above **EVERY** name on Heaven and Earth to speak over every circumstance. These are the benefits of being a Chosen Generation who has the Favor of God upon their lives. You have been given the power of the Holy Spirit to stand tall in Christ no matter what you may face. So today lift that head, brush that dirt off your shoulders and stand tall in Jesus. You are called and in you is the power to call down heaven on your behalf. So, just in case you forgot, you are the Kings kid. Stand up and show the enemy you are not defeated. God built you for such a time as this. March on soldier of God, march on

Affirmation:

Say this with me: Dear Lord, I thank you for the victory that you have given me and for the power to walk with my head held high, help me to remember to use the tools that are given to me to shut the enemy down, and to show the enemy that the weapon he formed against me didn't prosper. I am thankful for all you continue to do in me and through me. and in that Lord, I find my strength daily. Thank you for choosing me in Jesus name: Amen.

Notes:

Day 26

Keep seeking. you are about to find what you are looking for.

Ask, And It Shall be Given You: Seek, And Ye Shall Find: Knock, And It Shall Be Open Unto You; Matthew 7:7

Your pursuit will determine your real interest in that which you desire. When wanting something bad enough, many will travel to the ends of the earth to receive it. When I was on drugs and alcohol, I did whatever it took to get that which I was longing for. No matter how I felt, what was happening around me or what I did or didn't have, I was going to get the drugs my body needed no matter what. Imagine if we put that type of effort into the things of God when we seek Him for His Kingdom will in our lives. Some of us go to God with a ho-hum mindset, asking God, but not really pushing for the answer. We nonchalantly ask not really believing God will answer, then when He doesn't, we say "see I tried." But **Matthew 21:22** says: **And All Things, Whatsoever Ye Shall Ask In Prayer, Believing, Ye Shall Receive.** So, instead of letting your head or your heart, ask, seek, or knock, let your faith do it for you. The word says that **Faith The Grain Of A Mustard Seed Availeth Much. Luke 17:6.**

Prayer knocks on the door but it is faith that opens the it. Now another component of seeking is making sure it is of God's will for your life. **James 4:2-3** tells us **that we have not because we ask not, or we do ask but only for our own benefit and lustily desires (Paraphrase).** When we ask, seek, and knock we must do it lining up with the will of God and what is written in his word. Without praying in His Will in Faith, we are setting ourselves up not to receive from God. So, if you know its Gods will, keep seeking Him for it and don't let a non-answer discourage you. God will answer in due time, and He will grant you the partitions of your heart that are of His will. Keep pushing through, God replies to those who diligently seek Him.

Affirmation:

Say This with Me: Thank You Father, for always listening to me and supplying me with what I need. Help me to stand strong on your word when waiting on you to reply to my prayers. As I pray let me do it with the right motives and right heart. My faith is in you Lord and I know you can do all things but fail. So please forgive me if and when I waver or show any doubt. I place all my trust in you Lord and I know you will guide me and direct me in the way I should go. Thank you, Lord, for always listening to my prayers. In Jesus Precious Name: Amen

Notes:

Day 27

Bypass The Attitude And Do It With Gratitude.

Every an According As He Purposeth In His Heart, So Let Him Give, Not Grudgingly, Or Of Necessity: For God Loves A Cheerful Giver; 2 Corinthians 9:7

When starting your day today, begin it with prayer and worship unto the Lord. But when done doing so, let the next thing on your mind be "How can I be a blessing unto another today"? Then go through your day looking to be just that. See when you are about our Fathers business in ministering or helping others in time of need, You are then fulfilling the words Jesus spoke of when he said **I come to do the will of the Father who sent me: (John 6:38).** But also, as you do this don't do it as an obligation or for something you must check off a check list to get God's approval or attention. But do it as a cheerful giver of your time and or resources for the glory of God. See when we bless others with what God has given us with a cheerful heart and not doing it to expect a return, then you have fulfilled the will of God here on earth. When you make time for others, even though your day may be busy, or you give even though you may not have enough for yourself and you do it in the name of the Lord, God sees, and God is pleased, and your giving isn't done in vain.

Scripture says, **Everything you do, do it as you are doing it unto the Lord (Colossians 3:23).** It also says: **When you have done it for the least of them, you have done it unto me (Matthew 25:40).** So, take time even when you don't have it, and use your resources even when they may be running low, to bless another who may just need a shoulder to lean on or a meal to eat. We are blessed to be a blessing and when we are, God will continue to pour His blessings on you because you are using His blessings for His glory and not your own. Be ready today to be used by God and do it with your whole heart, no matter who it is He sends your way. Your blessings are waiting on the other side of your obedience. Today be a cheerful giver unto God and let Him be glorified in your life.

Affirmation

Say this with me: Father thank you for all the blessings, every provision, and every promise you have kept and made on my behalf. Help me not to not just be grateful but also generous with what you have placed in my hands. Remind me Lord that I have been placed here to your will and not my own. Help me to see those who are in need and then remember that those are the ones you are trying to reach. I thank you Lord for giving me the opportunity to be used by you. Let me be a representative of you in all I say and do. I thank you in advance Lord and give you all the praise. In Jesus name: Amen

Notes:

Day 28

You Did Not Create Me To Worry.

Be Careful For Nothing: But In Every Thing By Prayer And Supplication And Thanksgiving Let Your Request Be Made Known Unto God. And The Peace Of God, Which Surpasses All Understanding, Shall Keep Your Hearts And Minds Through Christ Jesus. Philippians 4:6:7

I know watching the news, listening to family members and co-workers, and looking at situations and circumstances around us can cause a little worry, fear, anxiety and or depression to creep into our lives. But beginning your day focused on Christ Jesus and the word of God can wash these fears away. God didn't create you to fear, but to trust and lean on Him in times of confusion and struggles. I know this can be a lot easier said than done. But it takes training up your faith to see beyond what is in front of you. You know David won the battle before he even faced Goliath. Reason being his faith allowed him to focus on God and not the giant. The enemy wants you to focus on the problem and not the problem solver. God wants you to trust Him. He is the same God who has made a way out of no way through everything you have faced in the past. And He is able do it again if you put your trust in Him.

God promised if you kept your mind on stayed on Him **(Jesus)** He would keep you in perfect peace. Not just peace, but Perfect Peace. That is Gods peace from above even in the midst of your struggles. You were not created to worry, but to trust. Trust God with every aspect of your life, the good and the bad and watch Him bring you through. So, focus on God and the sacrifice of His son Jesus, and the price He paid for you to make it through. You are a conquer in Christ and God will keep you in perfect peace if you seek Him in times of need. The Favor of God is upon you. Continue in that Favor and watch God move.

Affirmation:

Say this with me: Thank You Jesus for that perfect peace that surpasses all understanding. I thank You for the favor You have given me over the years. I know that it was You alone who has kept me in times past and is continuing to keep me now. Thank You for everything You do and have done on my behalf. You did not create worry, but you created me to put my trust in You, so today Lord I do just that. You are the Great I AM and there is nothing too hard for You. I am thankful and Grateful for all you do. In Jesus Holy Name: Amen

Notes:

Day 29

I Am Blessed

***Blessed Shalt Thou Be In The City, And Blessed Shalt
Thou Be In The Field.
Deuteronomy 28:3***

Hey you! Yes you. You are Blessed. It may not seem that way now, but you are. Stop listening to those things around you that are telling you differently. God said you are blessed, so take Him at His word. You are blessed, Mentally, Physically, Spiritually and Emotionally. You are blessed in the city, in the fields, in your workplace, in the marketplace and in your home. You are blessed coming and going and the blessings of the Lord are working in you and through you. This should be your daily affirmation and mindset no matter your situation. The word says **Death And Life Are In The Power Of The Tongue: And The That Love It Shall Eat The Fruit There Of. Proverbs 18:21**. You must begin to speak blessings and not curses over ourselves, our families and our situations in Life. Speaking life and not death, prosperity and not poverty and breakthroughs not bondage will be the difference between a life of blessings or a life of dread.

Let us start testifying more about the many blessings God has given us over the years and speak less about what the enemy is doing **We are Over-comers by the Blood of the Lamb and the word of our testimony in Him Revelations 12:11)**. Do you want to see more breakthroughs in your life? Begin to give God more praise than complaints and watch him begin pour out more blessings. God inhabits the praises of His people and when the praises go up the blessings come down. Begin to say you are blessed and put the enemy on notice that his weapons are not working. Because speaking life gives God power to move rather than speaking death and giving the enemy a foothold to have his way. So, proclaim to the enemy and yourself every day, I Am Blessed and Highly Favored. Because God promised it to those who serve Him and God doesn't sleep on His promises.

Affirmation:

Say this with me: Father God, thank You for Your mercy and grace that has kept me and Your continuous blessing that You have poured upon me time and time again, even when I didn't deserve them. I thank You Jesus for every breakthrough and deliverance, for things seen and unseen and for continued provision and protection against every weapon formed against me. Lord help me to see every blessing and remind me to give thanks for all You have done and do daily. I love You Lord and I am truly grateful for it all. In Jesus Mighty Name: Amen

NOTES:

Day 30

I will not let go Lord.

And He Said, Let Me Go, For The Day Breaketh. And He Said, I Will Not let Thee Go, Except Thou Bless Me. Genesis 32:26

In the story of **Genesis 32**, Jacob finally had enough of life and what he was facing. So, he decided to grab a hold of the Angel of God and said, "**I Will Not Let Go Until You Bless Me**". Question: Do you have a Jacob mindset today? Are you holding on to God with everything you have? Do you have a made- u p mind that no matter what happens you are not letting go of God? I pray the answers to these questions are yes, yes and yes. We all need to have a Jacob mindset and attitude towards God, that we will not let go until we see His blessings. But even after we have seen them, we are still hanging on because we know without Him, we will fail. Our strength, peace, joy, and breakthroughs are found in Christ, and we must reach out and grab a hold of Him with everything we have. Wonderful thing about this story was God didn't just change his circumstances, but He also changed his name. God is ready to change your name if you just hold on and not let go. All those things the enemy called you will no longer stick. For you are blessed of God and He said in **Matthew 10:22 that those who endure to the end shall be saved.**

In **James 1:12** Gods says: **Blessed is the man that endureth temptation: for when he is tried, he shall receive the crown of life**, which is promised to them that love Him. We must endure all that the enemy is throwing at us and trust and believe God for His promises and His provisions. The Word says: **I (you) can do all things through Christ who strengthens you Philippians 4:13**. which means Christ has given you the strength to hold on no matter what, even if it's just by the hem of His garment Don't Let Go! No matter what may come always remember, God has not forgotten or forsaken you. You are His and He will answer. Just continue to hold on.

Affirmation

Say this with me: Lord God, thank You for always remembering me and keeping me through every trial. Thank You Father for every promise you have made and ever provision you have kept concerning me. Even in my weakest times Lord, you have strengthened me and upheld me in Your mighty hands. I know my strength and my purpose is found in you, and if I am not connected to You, I will not fail. Keep me connected Lord so I may be who You called me to be and do what You have called me to do. I am the vine Lord, and You are the tree, and I will not let You go Lord because you are the source that sustains me. In Jesus Precious Name: Amen

Notes:

Thank You

Well, we are at the end of your 30-day journey, and I pray that you have received something to help you grow mentally and spiritually in the things of God and His will for your life. This Christian Walk isn't easy, I Know. But the more we learn, the more we grow in Him and our calling. God's word says in **Proverbs 27:17 Iron Sharpens Iron** so; I pray that this book has done just that for you. I Pray that it has helped you to seek God in every area of your life and adjust those things that are needed to carry out His goals and purpose for you. My hope is that the last 30 days has pushed you to dive deeper into His word and seek Him with your whole heart. For as His word says **Seek Him with Your whole heart and He shall be found (Jeremiah 29:13).** Thank you for your support and I pray that God continues to take you from Faith to Faith and Glory to Glory in Him. God bless and love you all.

Evangelist Jay Parker